My Financial Legacy

Rachael Freed

Published by MinervaPress, Minneapolis. For more information, please call (612) 558-3331, or visit our web site at www.life-legacies.com.

ISBN 978-0-9817450-7-7

Excerpted from 2012 edition of *Women's Lives, Women's Legacies* 978-0-9817450-0-8

Printed in the United States of America
First Edition: 2012

09 08 07 06 05 8 7 6 5 4 3 2

Cover design: Christopher Kirsh
Cover Photo: Djerba, Tunisia, El Ghriba Synagogue Olive Tree by Patty Shapiro

My Financial Legacy

It's surprising and confusing that most people have wills, many have living wills (health directives), and almost no one has an ethical will. How can we decide how we want our money, property and other worldly valuables to be dispersed if we haven't articulated our values and considered what matters most to us in our lives? How can we make legal decisions about our end-of-life care, including naming a representative to have power of attorney over our very lives, if we've not reflected on the purpose and legacy of our sacred lives?

To answer these questions and make wise choices about our money and our financial legacies, we'll first review. Then we'll reflect about the unique meaning of money in our lives and our choices and decisions about how to apportion our finances for our inheritors and for our philanthropic legacy.

Ethical wills preserve and communicate our values. Though not a legal document, the ethical will is a spiritual declaration for those who will come after you. It expresses who you were, what meant most in your life, your learning, love, and blessings for future generations, and how you want to be remembered after you're gone. An ethical will (legacy letter) differs from your living will, or health directive, that defines how you want to be cared for at the end of your life, and what a dignified end of life means to you. Your will of "valuables," is a legal declaration assigning your inheritors property and material "stuff". The ethical will, the non-legal complementary cousin of your legal will ("last will and testament") and your living will (health care directive), has its own purpose, but can and should inform your choices as you prepare your will and living will.

Now let's get back to money. Given the norms of our patriarchal culture, it's not surprising that many people think a woman's wealth lies in her heart and not her wallet. Yet women control 54 percent of the money in the United States. According to the census there were 7.8 million female business owners in America in 2007. Women handle money every day: earning, spending, saving, and giving.

Yet when it comes to financial decisions, too many women feel disenfranchised, especially if they have never been the primary or even secondary wage earners in their families. For them, the subject of money is more than uncomfortable; it may be terrifying.

If you're accustomed to delegating your financial decisions to your spouse or partner, take note: 53% of women are widowed by the age of 75. The average age of becoming a widow is 57. At some point your finances will become your responsibility. Whether you have $100 or $1,000,000, your legacy will be incomplete unless you decide how your money will be used when you are gone.

Many of us have the necessity of learning to master our finances at the same time as we face a major life crisis, a transition.

The two major crises (transitions) women face are: a diagnosis of a life-threatening illness, or loss of a spouse through death or divorce. It isn't new news that we are always in some kind of transition in our personal lives: life stages from childhood to old age, relationships, jobs, unemployment, and retirement.

All change has three components: first, the end or death of something; second, the in-between, the time of transition; and third, the rebirth or beginning of something new. The in-between, so rich in potential and the foundation of creativity, is also the most difficult, the loneliest and most terrifying component of change. We yearn for support, for clarity, for direction, for answers, for a way to feel "in control".

The past is over and the future not yet, but few of us consistently live in the present, especially when we're stressed. We're more likely to fret and worry or rush to make decisions to escape feeling lost and directionless. Whether the transition is benign and regular like the change of seasons of the year; or perhaps not always benign but expected, as we make the transition from one life stage to the next, living in the inbetween is hard and unsupported in our society.

A good policy when we find ourselves in a major life transition is to not make any major decisions for at least a calendar year. The first year after a loss or change is most successfully spent grieving the loss of the old, supported by family and friends. Gathering information about financial and all other decisions is also appropriate, including considering the help of professional advice and advisors. (See section: Choosing a Professional)

Caveat: Beware of those who want to sell you something, anything, especially when you're vulnerable: services, investments, insurance

No matter how unique our situation, we have in common the obligation of handling our money in our new circumstances and the responsibility to make decisions about how to allocate our money when we die.

Transition is not the only complication; another is the cultural taboo about money. In our society it is easier for people to talk about our values about dying and sex than it is to discuss or ask questions about money.

Using legacy principles we'll challenge outdated social taboos related to women and finance. You'll explore your own relationship with money, identify your attitudes and build your self-confidence.

Finally, we'll explore finding a trustworthy legacy advisor, planning your financial legacy, determining how much money you'll need for your future, how much to leave your heirs, and how much to contribute toward building a better world.

Women and Money

Esther Berger, a former PaineWebber vice president, observes that women's interest in money has been consistently discouraged, if not virtually disallowed, throughout history. "For centuries, at every turn and at every level, men made the money, and those who made it were permitted to own and control it. . . The deep-rooted presumption of masculine authority over money continues to hold women back and keep them afraid: afraid of earning money; afraid of understanding it; afraid, even, of confronting their fear of it."

Some women do not relate to this discomfort with money. These women control their finances and have negotiated mutually respectful financial relationships with their partners. They take pride in earning, saving, spending, and donating as they see fit, confident in their ability to handle money and to support themselves and their families.

The myth of money, of course, is that women don't know how to handle it, as if money had a gender.

– Frances Lear

Most women, however, have a certain amount of anxiety, shame, fear related to money. For many of us, even talking about money seems taboo. Perhaps we've been told throughout our lives that money is too complex for women to understand. Maybe somewhere deep inside we still believe that a handsome prince will sweep us up, ride away in his fancy convertible and take care of our financial needs forever. Too many of us have handed our power to a husband or partner, whether freely or under pressure, because we've never been taught otherwise.

4

We have found our voices in many areas of our lives.

With the goal of challenging our outdated perspectives, our habitual relationship with money and gaining power over our finances, let's roll up our sleeves and get to work.

REFLECTION AND WRITING

This exercise will help you identify your attitudes about finances. If you can, let go of the anxiety that may be your companion and replace it with a sense of objectivity, even playfulness. Most of us begin with deficits (pardon the pun) in this arena; some we are aware of and others we are not.

~ *Part 1*   *(10 to 15 minutes)*

Here is a list of words that refers to money: Acquisitive, Affluent, Afraid, Anxious, Appreciative, Benevolent, Big-hearted, Careful, Cautious, Charitable, Cheap, Comfortable, Compulsive, Confident, Conservative, Covetous, Economical, Empowered, Envious, Fearful, Foolish, Frugal, Generous, Grateful, Greedy, Hesitant, Hoarding, Ignorant, Impoverished, Impulsive, Indebted, Irresponsible, Knowledgeable, Lavish, Liberal, Miserly, Modest, Obsessive, Openhanded, Philanthropic, Poor, Possessive, Prosperous, Protective, Prudent, Responsible, Rich, Self-indulgent, Selfish, Sensible, Spendthrift, Stingy, Thrifty, Wasteful, Wealthy, Well informed, Wise, Worried.

Circle three words that describe your positive relationship with money. Next, underline three words that describe negative aspects of your relationship with money. Finally, place a check mark next to three words that you wish described your relationship with money. If you think of a word not on the list that falls into one of these categories, add it.

Read the lists aloud to yourself. If you have a trusted friend or financial advisor, read your lists to her.

Write about your habits and attitudes related to earning, saving, spending, and giving. Consider the following:

- Return to your lists in part 1. How do the words in each list relate to your financial attitudes and habits?
- Are you satisfied or discouraged with your saving pattern? With your spending behaviors? With your giving habits?
- How do your values match up with your perspectives and beliefs about money?
- Are there people with whom you can comfortably talk about how you feel about money – your partner or spouse, your children, siblings, parents, friends, your financial advisor, other professionals?

My Money Training

As a product of my generation, I still hear echoes of "don't worry your pretty little head about it" from the 1950s and "money's dirty" from I'm not sure where. This makes me afraid of money, of being dumb. And if I'm smart about money, then will I still be considered feminine?

I recall feeling humiliated when a solicitor told me how much I "should" give to her charitable organization. She knew nothing about my circumstances. At the time my husband was in graduate school and we were living on my teacher's salary. Unable to give, I felt ashamed and beat a hasty retreat to my shelter of choice: contempt for the solicitor and her organization that lasted decades.

Years later, after my financial situation had improved, I felt another kind of shame. I was riding the subway in New York when a pregnant homeless woman entered the car. I immediately looked away. As she walked through the car, begging unsuccessfully, she began a furious tirade that silenced us all. She said that it was okay if we didn't give her money, she just wanted someone to look her in the eyes and acknowledge her existence, because she was a human being too. She then strode, outraged, into the next car. I was stunned. For the first time I saw how my discomfort could lead to inhumane behavior. I vowed never again to avoid eye contact with a person less fortunate than I.

In my thirties – the height of my disdain – I fantasized about leaving civilization and going to live in the woods, where I wouldn't have to deal with money. I had just returned from serving in the Peace Corps, living amid people for whom lifelong poverty was a reality. Paradoxically, I now found myself riding in a golf cart at the country club that my husband and I had joined. Conflicted, I had to let go of my fantasy. Avoiding money would make no difference in a world of plenty where children go hungry. I let go of the country club as well, ashamed at participating in such expensive exclusivity.

I've joked about my acquisitive habits, my inability to resist clever marketing techniques, my tendency to impulse-buy. But I'm working seriously, and slowly, on simplifying my life. I fantasize about how wealthy I'll be when the world economy fails. With my collection of stunning stones and carefully picked seashells, I'll have lots to barter with.

For me, money has been an uncomfortable topic – and I'm not alone. As women, we know that our experience with our families and society shaped our early perceptions about money. Nevertheless, when we examine our personal financial histories today, we are often surprised at the negative feelings that arise.

Stay involved with your money, for what happens to your money affects the quality of your life and the lives of all those you love.
– Suze Orman

What you've learned about money – is a mirror image that reflects the attitudes, values, and beliefs of the people and society that raised you...this childhood training affects us deeply.
– Ruth Hayden

Get comfortable in your sacred writing space, then think of as many memories related to money as you can. Use the following questions to stimulate your reflection. Then, write about your experiences with money, letting your memory guide you. Because of the emotionality of this topic, consider writing your thoughts on one side of the paper and feelings on the other. You may need to set aside your writing and come back to it after a day or even two. Several short writing sessions can accomplish your goal just as well as one long session.

- What were your earliest experiences with money? Did you perceive a lack of or an abundance of money in your family as you grew up? Did you have an allowance? Were you paid to do certain chores? If you received money as a child, were you given guidelines about how to use it? Were you expected to share your money or give any of it to help others? Did you consider the money "yours"?

- Reflect on your family's explicit and implicit attitudes about money. How do you feel about this inherited legacy? In what ways were your parents positive and negative role models for earning, saving, spending, and giving? In what ways do you handle money like your mother? Like your father?

- Have you inherited money? Are these funds separate from your everyday finances? How do you use or invest the money you've inherited? Do you make charitable contributions with this money?

- Consider your experiences with money as an adult – areas of comfort and discomfort, conflict and harmony, secrecy and openness. Do you generally believe that you are blessed with abundance, or do you feel the pinch of scarcity?

- How do you get money? If you have a partner, how does money affect your relationship? Do you make financial decisions alone, with a partner, or with others in your family?

- Are you comfortable spending money on yourself for your basic needs? For luxuries? For fun? Are you generous or stingy with yourself? What are your limits for spending on yourself?
- Do you spend money on others? Do you regularly buy gifts for those you love? Do you give money to others? How do you decide how much to spend or give?
- Have you ever given to charitable causes or to individuals less fortunate than you? Why or why not? Have you ever given to a homeless person? To someone begging? How do you feel about being asked for money? How do you decide how much, to whom, and when you will give? Do you make charitable contributions as a family? How do you decide on amounts and recipients?

Sometimes perspectives and assumptions are clarified by reading aloud or sharing with another. If you have a trusted friend or financial advisor who you believe will be kind and understanding, decide whether to share part or all of your writing. Sharing with a woman you trust can help you hone your direction, refine your insight, deepen your compassion, and strengthen your power.

Money you have beyond what you need for survival is either bondage or freedom.
– Mitchell Chefitz

Saving and investing for our future may be the only way to predict our future.
– Frances Lear

Anticipating My Financial Needs

We are often told, in this day and age, that we must take care of ourselves if we expect to care for others. But society teaches women to give, give, give, and we've been well trained. We have a lot to learn about self-care.

This, coupled with our taboos concerning money, makes it challenging to consider our personal financial needs for the future. But unless we plan for ourselves, we will not be adequately prepared to consider the financial legacies we wish to leave.

REFLECTION AND WRITING

~ *Part 1*   *(30 minutes)*

Visualize yourself at a time in the future – five, ten, even twenty-five years from now. No matter your age, marital status, or financial situation today, imagine that you are financially independent. Write about what you see, using the following prompts:

- What is your monetary situation? What kind of lifestyle do you have? How are you maintaining this lifestyle?
- What are your personal care needs and healthcare costs?
- What are you spending your money on? Do you have adequate funds to meet your basic needs? Do you have additional money for books, travel, restaurants, and other luxuries?
- Can you go where you want, do what you want, buy what you want?
- Has your budget shrunk or increased in the last decade?

Now, return to the present moment and write about your experience.

- What surprised you about your trip into the future?
- What can you do today to prepare for the future?
- How will you ensure that you'll have what you need as you age?
- Are there attitudes about money that you want to change? How can you make these changes?
- Do you need counsel, perhaps from a trusted friend, a professional, a financial advisor?

~ *Part 2*   *(no time limit)*

Write out a plan for your financial future, a blueprint for action. Since this is new territory for many women, share your ideas with someone you trust – a friend or family member. You may want to seek advice and support from a financial professional as you begin to plan for your financial future.

Handling the Inheritance

Unless we make specific arrangements, our money will automatically be distributed according to state probate laws after we die. For some women this may be acceptable, but most feel strongly about determining where their money will go.

Many women leave some money for loved ones, generally their children or grandchildren. The question of whether and how much to give, however, is complex. Your choices range from leaving the maximum possible inheritance, regardless of need, to no inheritance at all. You may want to consider how you want the money to be used – in a manner consistent with your values or at your heirs' discretion. You may need to find a creative way to communicate your preference.

Carol, a single woman and lifelong professional, decided to leave part of her estate to her three nieces and her nephew. Because she had strong feelings about making a difference in the community, she wanted to bequeath a spiritual message as well. Carol believed that her heirs would come to understand the importance of giving not through her words, but through their own experience. So, working with professionals to set up her estate, she stipulated that a percentage of the annual payout would go to the charitable cause of each heir's choice. She then used her ethical will, knowing it is not a legal document, to explain her values and what she hoped to accomplish with her gift.

Next we'll explore options for distributing your financial legacy. You will explain to your loved ones how you arrived at your decisions and which values you hope to impart along with your money. This is a multi-faceted aspect of your legacy work. It requires creativity to use your money in a way that integrates your values with your desire to give. Further, it demands the courage to voice your decisions straightforwardly in writing. This challenge is about your self-respect and integ-

Leave children enough to do anything, but not enough to do nothing. – Warren Buffet

rity. Your intellect, your values, and your deepest spiritual beliefs will guide these important decisions.

REFLECTION AND WRITING

~ *Part 1*   *(15 to 30 minutes)*

Many people, among them the very wealthy, plan to distribute most of their wealth to charitable causes rather than to their children. They cite numerous reasons: handing money to the children may do more harm than good; if the kids earn it themselves, they'll develop an appreciation for it; it's more important to contribute to healing the problems of society. When substantial amounts of money are involved, some parents express concern about their children's self esteem if they don't need to work to support themselves. In these cases, many people decide on an upper limit for their children's inheritance. Beyond that amount, they plan to contribute their money where it will do the most good.

Other parents feel a strong obligation to their children. They have supported and protected their children all their lives, and they see no reason to stop after their deaths. These people hope to give their heirs a leg up: providing a safety net, a down payment on a house, college tuition for grandchildren. They trust their children to use the money responsibly.

Take time to review your earlier writings. With your values firmly in mind, write your preliminary thoughts about giving – or not giving – to loved ones. Stay within the time limit, and write for as many days as needed until you have fully explored the subject and feel ready to move forward.

~ *Part 2*   *(30 to 60 minutes)*

If you have decided not to leave a portion of your financial legacy to loved ones, skip this step and move on to part 3. Otherwise, use the allotted time to explore the following:

- How much money do you want to leave to your family: some, most, or all of it? Be as candid and truthful as you can be with yourself.
- Consider how you will distribute your money among your heirs. Take into account: age, a child with special needs, a child more successful than your others. Consider how these factors influence your decisions about inheritance. In this world of blended families, will you differentiate between your own children and your stepchildren?
- If you distribute the money equally, what are your reasons? If you divide the inheritance according to need or other considerations, what issues might this raise among your heirs?
- Are you envisioning gifting a portion of your financial legacy to people other than your children and grandchildren? Nieces, nephews, nonrelatives? On what basis will you make this decision?
- What values do you want to pass on with your money? Do you want to influence the use of the inherited money? Do you want to ensure that a portion of the inheritance is tithed annually to charitable causes?
- Is this money an outright gift? Is it a reward for your loved ones' values and achievements? How would you feel if one or more of your heirs failed to handle their inheritance in a responsible way? Why do you want your heirs to have this money?
- How do you want to distribute this money, in one payment or a planned amount over time? Will you designate trustees to oversee distribution? Will you set the money aside until your heirs reach a certain age? Will you distribute part or all of this money before your death?
- How might this inheritance complicate your loved ones' values or life challenges?

~ *Part 3*   *(30 to 60 minutes)*

Now that you've thoroughly explored your reasons for giving or not giving, write a letter explaining how you arrived at your decisions. If you are giving any portion of your financial legacy to loved ones, be sure to discuss the values you hope to impart with your gift. Then set this letter aside with the other materials to be included in your legacy document and to use as a guide for writing your will.

And of all that You give me,
will set aside a tithe for You.
— Gen. 28:22

Service is the rent we pay for
room on this planet.
— Shirley Chisholm

…get behind a cause and pass
it down through generations…
your fire from within.
— Dr. Musimbi Kanyoro,
CEO, Global Fund for
Women

[S]he who saves a life, it is as
though [s]he has saved the
world entire.
— The Talmud

Leaving Money to Charitable Causes

"Tikkun Olam," a concept from Jewish mystical tradition, means "repairing the world." How did the world become in need of repair? We're told that God tried to contain the holy light, the first creation, in vessels. But the light was so powerful that the vessels burst and shattered. Discord and confusion spread as the light flew to every corner of the universe. So, God created us as partners, challenging us to find and collect the shards of light and repair the broken world.

Contributing to charitable causes is one of many ways to repair the world, something that Elena, a sculptor, tried to keep in mind when she unexpectedly received a large inheritance. First she decided how much she would need for herself, then she determined how much she wanted to pass on to her children. But when she thought she was ready to contribute a percentage of her inheritance to her church community, she was unable to sign the documents. She'd come up against an issue she'd struggled with all her life: fear of losing control. Finally she sought counsel with her spiritual advisor, who asked, "How will the world be better because you've lived?" With these words Elena was able to move forward, integrating her need for control with her strong commitment to do what she could to repair the world. She met with the development professional at her church, and together they worked out a plan allowing her to direct the church's use of her contribution. Taking a hands-on approach to make a difference in the world became a personally empowering – and spiritually satisfying – part of Elena's legacy.

Giving is a spiritual act, one that feels natural to many women. We give our time, effort, and heart; we spend countless hours stamping envelopes, making telephone calls, feeding the homeless, and assisting families in crisis. We give so much that the annual 8.1 billion volunteer hours in the United States is currently valued at $173 billion.

Our tendency to give of ourselves is only a hop, skip, and jump from giving money, so it's no surprise that more and more women are finding ways to use their money to repair the world. We are beginning to shift our thinking, to empower ourselves, to realize that our financial contributions make an impact.

Giving to charitable causes is not just an opportunity for the rich; it's something anyone can do. As little as we may have, there are always those who have less. To quote a Minnesota schoolteacher, "My estate will never be large enough to be able to build libraries, but it may be large enough to buy some books for a library."

Give of yourself.... No one has ever become poor from giving.
— Anne Frank

For many of us, charitable giving is of the utmost importance. If we don't make charitable bequests, we surrender our last chance to make a difference in the world. Worse, unless we have a legal will, some or all of our funds may go by default to the government. Then our money may be used to develop weapons of mass destruction or drilling for oil in the wilderness, when we wanted it to feed children, shelter abused women, protect endangered species, fund the arts, or support education.

REFLECTION AND WRITING

~ *Part 1*   *(30 to 90 minutes)*

You are no doubt committed to any number of social or political causes. To determine where your money will do the most good, you will need to consider what, specifically, you want your financial legacy to accomplish. For example, if you feel passionate about supporting education, you might focus on literacy, tutoring, scholarships, adult learning, diversity programs, a lecture series, electronic devices for media centers, or programs to encourage young women in math and science.

Next, you'll need to seek out organizations that might be a good fit. The Internet offers a wealth of information, and most organizations provide Web sites displaying their mission statements and other details. Here are some of the causes that you might want to explore: Animal welfare, arts and culture, children and families, church and religious organizations, civil rights, death and dying, economic and social justice, education, environment, ethics, GLBT rights, "green" living, health and medicine, homelessness, hunger, international relief and development, media and freedom of expression, peace and human rights, religion and spirituality, scientific research, seniors, veterans and their families, violence against women and children, women's opportunities, and women's rights.

Before making a donation, be sure to investigate an organization's credibility and fiscal responsibility, and find out exactly how your money will be used.

To get started in your research, you might contact Charity Navigator or the Better Business Bureau Wise Giving Alliance. Both organizations offer descriptions of various nonprofits, assistance in evaluating organizations, and credible reports on charities in the United States and abroad. Charity Navigator includes Tips for Savvy Givers such as "what to look for" and "concentrate your giving."

Charity Navigator
www.charitynavigator.org

Better Business Bureau Wise Giving Alliance
www.bbb.org/us/charity

Here's what some women say about why they make charitable gifts: To fulfill my life purpose, to leave an imprint on society, to make a significant difference, to do my part to heal the world, to feel like my life has made a difference, to fulfill a responsibility in my faith community, to perpetuate my philosophy or perspective, to give back in gratitude for the abundance I'm privileged to have, to deepen my spiritual life and commitment, to help my favorite charity accomplish its mission, to memorialize and honor my family and ethnic group, to establish my immortality, to connect with others who share my passions and interests, to experience the satisfaction of knowing I've done something worthwhile.

Once you determine how much you want to give and to whom, you'll need professional assistance to draw up a legal will to document your gifts. (See "Choosing a Professional" below.) But first, take as much time as you need to write about your reasons for giving. Do this for yourself, for your professional advisor, and, most important, for the recipients of your ethical will. Your loved ones will value a clarification of your goals and decisions. They'll appreciate knowing how you integrated your financial legacy with your love for them and your passion to repair the world.

Begin by listing the reasons for your decisions. Then, use the letter-writing technique to expand on your list. Writing a legacy letter to accompany your legal will is an opportunity to express how and why you made your choices. A legacy letter makes talking about money, our last taboo, easier for you and your potential survivors and inheritors. Include examples, descriptions, and anecdotes. Address your letter to those who will inherit your financial legacy. When you're finished, file this letter with your other materials for your ethical will.

Choosing a Professional

To legitimize your financial gifts, and to clarify the legality of your decisions, you will need the help of a professional advisor. Remember, your ethical will does not take the place of a legal document. In order to ensure the distribution of your financial legacy according to your plan, you must provide for it legally.

For many women, this means venturing into what seems an alien, hostile world. To choose an advisor, first ask your women friends or family for referrals. Often another woman's satisfaction is a good place to begin your research. The Certified Financial Planners Board is a nationally recognized organization that grants the CFP designation to advisors who have undergone rigorous learning and testing in various financial planning fields. That's a good first step, but not enough.

The initials CFP behind an advisor's name may connote competence, but it doesn't certify her ability to listen, nor does it indicate that the two of you are "a fit" and can build a relationship of trust and confidence that you want to grow over years. Choosing your financial advisor is as important as choosing your surgeon or gynecologist. You want an advisor who has sensitivity, who will answer all your questions with respect, and is committed to her work. Armed with passionate

A sphere is made up of not one, but an infinite number of circles; women have diverse gifts, and to say that women's sphere is the family circle is a mathematical absurdity.

– Maria Mitchell

purpose, thoughtful planning, and what you have already reflected about and written, you can walk confidently into the office of an estate planner, a financial advisor, an attorney, or accountant.

Be sure to interview several advisors before choosing one. Here are some practical questions to ask:

1. Tell Me About Your Ideal Client

   A good financial advisor will have an area of expertise. Find a financial advisor whose ideal client sounds very similar to your situation in terms of age, stage of life, life situation, and asset level.

2. How Are You Compensated?

   If the advisor is paid directly by fees from you, a fee-only financial advisor, then she will have an incentive to provide advice and service that fits your goals. If she is paid by commission, or through a broker, then she is committed to selling the products her broker sells.

3. Ask An Advisor to Explain A Financial Concept To You

   If she speaks over your head or her answer makes no sense, then move on. You want to work with someone who can explain financial concepts to you in language you can understand. One sample question is: what are the advantages of annuities?

Remember, you are in a powerful position as a potential customer. Be especially wary of professionals who maintain an uncomfortable distance by using technical or exclusive language, who have their own agenda or interests, who trivialize your concerns, or whose ethics you question. The person you choose should listen and communicate well, treat you with respect, be willing to question and advise you while supporting your legacy choices. If you feel nervous about the initial meeting, you might ask a trusted friend to accompany you. Give yourself permission to hire someone else if your first choice doesn't work out.

Once you begin working with a professional advisor, be honest about who you are and what you're trying to do. If you don't understand something, ask for clarification. Don't sell yourself short: there are no stupid questions, and every question deserves a respectful answer.

As you work with your advisor, you may decide to keep a journal of your thoughts about this challenging subject. You may also want to document your growing self-confidence as you work with the energy of money – to include in your ethical will. What a wonderful gift for your daughters and granddaughters, who, in a different time, will consider such writing historical, just as we today view the writings by women who fought for the vote more than ninety years ago.

Dear Kristi and Ben,

What a waste of time shame is! A book I read long ago about shame starts with this sentence: "Shame is the invisible dragon that takes away our ability to speak."

One thing I rarely speak about is the foreclosure of our house on Luverne. There are many reasons, many excuses and many circumstances which preceded it, but the result was the bank taking our house back, our equity lost and credit rating compromised. Because your dad and I held the mortgage together, both of us had rejected applications and contracts and general money troubles for seven years.

Your dad managed to own two other houses and we managed to rent from friends of friends who didn't do credit checks. I leased a car because I couldn't buy one. I was able to co-sign college loans with you because the government counted on getting their money back from one of us. All of these complications caused me great shame: "what a bad person I am for defaulting on a mortgage and having so many strangers view me as untrustworthy."

This subject can still cause me visceral pain when I think about it. I haven't owned a house since, although I have never missed a rent or house sharing payment. If I only focus on shame, the other reality is lost to me. We were never homeless; we were never without a car or an earned income. You went to college with help from both parents. We did not go without.

The things that matter most – home, family and leisure time together is an enviable life. I'm very proud of how we did that and my wish for you is that if there is any shame for you in this life we led, you will let it go and rejoice with me in our abundance.

– Love, Mom

My dear daughter Scarlett,

As a child I sat cross-legged and stared for hours at the glossy gifts that lay waiting for me beneath the Christmas tree. Often my exuberance got the best of me. I remember the night my sister and I meticulously unwrapped our electric toothbrushes, brushed until sparkly clean, giggling uncontrollably as we taped them up again before our parents caught us.

At my father's funeral one man shared a story of how my dad gifted him with money so he could follow his dream to attend seminary. Another told of the time my dad slipped him extra pay for his work as a farmhand. My father's only caveat was, "This is just between you and me, my son."

It was a gift to be part of a family that could afford to shower me and others with presents, but not all the children in my rural community were so fortunate. Sometimes I learned the hard way, like when out of what I thought was jealousy, a friend stole my new winter boots. My child's heart did not understand, and I felt alone, confused, and out of place.

Later in life I learned that I was fortunate to live in a country where education was encouraged and medical care was readily accessible. I found cues in photographs and books that depicted a different way of life: famine, starving children, orphaned babies. As my world expanded. I remembered the child who stole my boots. My heart opened.

That's why in 2007 I answered, "Yes!" to an invitation to travel to Malawi, Africa, one of the ten poorest countries in the world. That decision changed my life.

Eighteen months later I returned to Malawi with a group of nine. We brought a multitude of gifts with us: Tylenol, aspirin, condoms, bandages, books, soccer balls, and more. There were no shiny wrappings to rip off, but the gratitude from those who received was palpable. They meant that an elderly arthritic woman in the village could sleep through the night and that an HIV/AIDS or malaria patient would find short-term relief from pain and fever. These gifts offered temporary respite from the harsh life in an impoverished country.

I don't know which was more powerful: the passion for giving or the receptivity of those who received. Somewhere along the journey, the line between giver and receiver blurred. Our group made a pact to continue working to empower girls and women near and far.

May you, my precious daughter, be blessed to receive and pass forward the seeds of generosity my father planted in my soul so long ago.

– Love, Mom

Notes

Appendix

Template for Writing a One-Page Legacy Letter and a Sample Letter

By the 12th century the traditional ethical will, men transmitting values to their sons, had taken the form of a written letter. Writing ethical wills is a natural undertaking for women today. We are the concerned storytellers who build, maintain and sustain family, community, and civilization.

Each of our ethical wills is unique. For many women a one-page legacy letter will be adequate or even perfect. Others may decide that each of her loved ones deserves a letter of their own. Still other women may continue to write legacy letters for a variety of purposes, to:
- commemorate special occasions, holidays or special birthdays
- express gratitude and celebrate life
- provide family history
- express values, love and blessings
- share life lessons, successes, regrets, disappointments
- tell the story of precious possessions
- make amends, ask forgiveness, share secrets
- request preferences for end-of-life care and ways to be remembered
- explain decisions in our legal documents: health directives, wills

I usually suggest that writers use timers, and limit writing to fifteen minutes, an amount of time that demands focus but is not so lengthy that one can excuse themselves with "not having the time". Women are always amazed at what can be accomplished in so short a time. Their amazement surprises me when we are so accomplished as multi-taskers!

Whatever the content, a template provides a structure to make writing legacy letters easier. A one page fifteen minute letter can be accomplished in four paragraphs.

Paragraph 1: Provide history and context. One of my mentors once said, "All texts have a context." We are seldom aware that the context beyond our personal lives affects us. The time when family history was contained in a family Bible and passed down from generation to generation is long gone. An opening paragraph to give the reader a snippet of family history and a snapshot of the historical times enriches what follows.

Paragraph 2: Tell the story. All of us have a sacred story, and all of us want to tell our stories. We feel known and have a sense of belonging when others listen attentively to our stories.

Paragraph 3: State the lesson learned. Learning from our experience is often defined as wisdom. It's this learning that we want to preserve and pass forward to future generations along with our love.

Paragraph 4: Offer a blessing. Your blessing flows naturally to your loved ones from your story and your learning. We're not always aware of the importance of being blessed, but we all need blessings from our elders.

The ancient ethical will was born out of the story of Jacob blessing his twelve sons (though not his daughter, Dina) as he lay dying at the end of the book of Genesis. That same Jacob earlier stole his father Isaac's blessing from his older brother, Esau. Esau's response was a plea to his father, in my opinion the most poignant words in Genesis: (27:38) "Have you but one blessing, my father? Bless me, even me also….And Esau lifted up his voice and wept."

Women too have the power to bless future generations. We're no different today. All of us need to be blessed, in our modern day, and as adults. We never outgrow our need for blessings! We experience being blessed as we bless future generations.

Here is a sample using the template: context, story, learning, blessing. I wrote this letter to my grown children after I read somewhere about "looking into people's faces when you pass them," that prompted a memory of my 1961 experience.

Dear Sid and Debbie,

In the summer of 1961, your Dad graduated from Officers Candidate School and began three years of service in the US Coast Guard. He was stationed at the Battery, at the south end of Manhattan. We sublet a ground-floor apartment on West 95th Street just half a block from Central Park in Spanish Harlem. At 22, I was optimistic, confident, and naively fearless. My job that summer was to find a teaching position for the fall.

One day on my way to some exciting adventure in the city, I got on the subway. I sat down and began to read. A pregnant, homeless woman entered the car, and began to beg for money. I averted my eyes, buried my face in my book, and clasped my heart and my purse tightly. Silent minutes passed and suddenly the woman began to shout at the riders – crying out that it was okay if we didn't give her money, but it wasn't okay to avoid looking her in the face – that she was a human being! She picked up her bags and lurched through the door into the next train car.

I was shocked and shamed. Since then, even when I choose not to give to a person begging, I look the person in the eye. I feel more human when I acknowledge another's humanity.

So, my beloved and precious children, Sid and Debbie, May you both be blessed with compassionate and wise eyes: eyes that see beyond the face of circumstance, that see the spark of the Divine deep within yourself, each other, and everyone on our planet.

I love you, Mom

A Sample Legacy Tips&Tools: The Legacy of Giving

Legacy Tips&Tools. a monthly one page e-newsletter, is free and can be subscribed to on www.life-legacies.com. In August 2009, the Tips was titled The Legacy of Giving. It described my plan to get my teenaged grandchildren involved in charitable giving. The reflection is always followed by suggestions for Action called: Principles of Practice.

The Legacy of Giving

Reflection:

Ethical wills are about our values, not our money. But what we think and do with money, how we use it, to whom or whether we give it, is part of our legacy of values. People are more open about sex and death than about money, which may be our last taboo. Though challenging, let's look at the relationship of money, values and legacy.

Here are some questions to consider:
How do you decide what to spend your money on?
What percentage of your money do you spend, save, invest in your own future and the future of the next generations?
How do you decide to whom & how much to give to "charitable causes"?
What's the legacy you intend to leave with your money?
What legacy are you leaving by the way you manage your money?
What values do you model with your legacy of giving?

Though most Americans give to charities on an annual basis, only about 15% of us translate that value into a philanthropic plan. I want my grandchildren (now five to fourteen years old) to be among those who normally think and act philanthropically. As part of my legacy to them, I devised this plan: to offer them money each year to be given to charity. Here in more detail is how we began.

In June of this summer I initiated the first phase of the "plan" with my two oldest grand-children. I called each, a girl fourteen and a boy thirteen, explaining that I had a proposal and wondered if I could take them to dinner to discuss it. Very grown up, they accepted my invitation and we went to a quiet restaurant to eat and talk.

Here's what I proposed to them: My intention is to provide you with money: this year $300 to give to charitable causes. It will be your responsibility together to decide to whom the money should be given. (As each of the other five cousins become teenagers, they'll be included and the annual amount will increase.) I hope you'll share your personal priorities with each other after thinking and doing any necessary research – discussing, debating, and deciding together who will receive the money.

If you want to consult with me at any time, I'm available. I plan for us to have dinner again before school starts in the fall. You can share your experience then, advise me of your decisions and I'll write the checks for your 2009 charitable gifts. We'll repeat this every summer.

After lively conversation, they agreed not to divide the money in half and each choose for themselves, but to engage with each other to research, discuss, and decide how much to give to whom. I was especially pleased by their willingness to work together. Beyond wanting them to experience gratitude for their blessings and to translate that into generosity, a responsible practice of giving, I want the cousins and siblings to be bonded.

I envision this giving as a way to enrich their relationships as they grow up, continuing to work together to think, discuss, decide and act every year on behalf of those less fortunate than they. (To that end, I am amending my will to include funds for this project in perpetuity.)

Their enthusiasm, their serious sense of responsibility, and their grasp of the scope and complexity of what they were undertaking was inspiring. After our discussion I provided a document – a sacred agreement – explaining what we'd discussed and agreed to. They felt very grown up signing it and we each have a copy. I also gave them journals for their note-taking and planning.

This story is far from complete. What's real is only phase one of year one. No stories or results to share – yet. Whatever they do, however they decide, they will have succeeded for the first time, and they'll have another opportunity next June when we meet again.

Principles of Practice:

1. Consider a value you have that you want to communicate and pass on.
2. Write about how you came to have this value and how you have lived it.
3. Translate the value into an action plan to make it part of your legacy. (It may be writing your experience, your learning, and your hopes and dreams for future generations.)
4. If you choose a value about charitable giving, and if a version of my plan interests you, please use it as is, or tweak it to meet your needs - make it yours…imagine if there were hundreds of thousands of young teens spending part of their summer looking for beneficiaries of charitable dollars.

May you be blessed by translating your values into lessons, into action, into love.

The Ethical Will: A New Tool To Help Women Givers
by Rachael Freed

Excerpted and revised: from Minnesota Law and Politics, March 2001

Women control 54% of the money in the U.S. and have great potential to influence the future of philanthropy and charitable giving. Yet this vast market is generally untapped. Why? Because methods developed for men don't address the needs of women.

Our knowledge about how women differ from men (beyond biology) suggests new approaches to this powerful, unrealized market. One of these, a contemporary transformation of an ancient tradition, is the "ethical will."

Preparing an ethical will helps women define values, explore family and cultural traditions, as well as clarify unique interests and passions. Whether a woman has great wealth or is of modest means, is a widow or divorcee, is successful in the marketplace, or a recipient of family inheritance, laying a foundation of values prior to constructing an estate or philanthropic plan is essential.

For women, charity has always been more than just about money. It's long been the norm for women to nurture by giving their time and energy, and to leave the charitable donations to men. Our cultural taboo about talking about money and the idea that money isn't feminine limit women's vision and suppress their charitable impulses.

Once connected to her history and to her unique life experience, a woman can match her values with a philanthropic cause and fund what reflects her individuality. Women leaving a legacy need to answer the question: How will my financial legacy make a difference for future generations? Funding legacies can accomplish women's goals to care for those in need, maintain human culture, strengthen community life, and protect all life on our planet.

Women want to influence the future. Estate planners, attorneys and accountants can be valuable and valued partners in the significant work of bringing women's financial legacies to fruition.

Rachael Freed is the author of *Women's Lives, Women's Legacies: Passing Your Beliefs and Blessings to Future Generations*, and *The Legacy Workbook for the Busy Woman: A Step-by-Step Guide for Writing an Ethical Will in Two Hours or Less*. Contact Freed, who develops and facilitates train the trainer programs, consults with estate planners, attorneys, development officers, charitable organizations, faith institutions, and groups, individuals and couples about legacies.

Bibliography

Arnold, Elizabeth. *Creating the Good Will: The Most Comprehensive Guide to Both the Financial and Emotional Sides of Passing on Your Legacy.* New York: Penguin Group, 2005.

Bridges, William. *Transitions: Making Sense of Life's Changes.* San Francisco: Da Capo Press, Perseus Books Group, 1980, 2004.

Brown, Judith N., and Christina Baldwin. *A Second Start: A Widow's Guide to Financial Survival at a Time of Emotional Crisis.* New York: Simon and Schuster, Fireside, 1986.

Dungan, Nathan. *Money Sanity Solutions.* Minneapolis: Share Save Spend, 2010.

Freed, Rachael A. *The Legacy Workbook for the Busy Woman: A Step-By-Step Guide for Writing a Spiritual-Ethical Will in Two Hours or Less.* Minneapolis: MinervaPress, 2005, 2012.

_____. *Women's Lives, Women's Legacies: Passing Your Beliefs and Blessings to Future Generations, Creating Your Own Ethical Will.* Minneapolis: MinervaPress, 2003, 2012.

Hayden, Ruth L. *How to Turn Your Money Life Around: The Money Book for Women.* Deerfield Beach, Fla.: Health Communications, 1992.

Kass, Amy A. ed. *Giving Well, Doing Good: Readings for Thoughtful Philanthropists.* Indianapolis: Indiana University Press, 2008.

Kay, Barbara A. and Anthony Di Leonardi. *The $14 Trillion Woman.* 2009.

Lear, Frances. Lear Magazine, April 1994.

Needleman, Jacob. *Money and the Meaning of Life.* New York: Doubleday, 1991.

Orman, Suze. *Women & Money: Owning the Power to Control Your Destiny.* New York: Spiegel and Grau/Random House, 2007.

Phillips, Michael, and Salli Rasberry. *The Seven Laws of Money.* New York: Random House, Word Wheel, 1974.